If Not for These Wrinkles of Darkness
Rembrandt: A Self-Portrait

If Not for These Wrinkles of Darkness
Rembrandt: A Self-Portrait

Stephen Frech

White Pine Press • Buffalo, New York

Acknowledgments:

Ascent: "The Green Crawler Finds its Way"

Florida Review: "The Windmill"

High Plains Literary Review: "Cornelia II" and "To Live This Close To Deer"

Literature and Belief: "I Would Be Clad in Christ's Skin"

Permafrost: "Female Nude of a Woman I've Never Seen Naked"

Pleiades: "The Bricklayer's Sled"

Rhino: "Rembrandt in the Studio with Pupils

River Styx: "The Hog" and "Self-Portrait with Saskia: The Prodigal Son in the Tavern"

Spoon River Poetry Review: "Return of the Lost Son," "Woman Bathing," and "The Adoration
of the Shepherds"

Sunstone: "Who'd Have Thought the Owl So Fierce" and "Hendrickje Stoffels"

"Letter to Cornelis Anslo, 1641" was printed as a broadside by Goshen College.

"Return of the Lost Son," "Simeon in the Temple," "The Denial of Peter," and "Descent from the Cross" are
part of the chapbook *Toward Evening and the Day Far Spent* that won the 1995 Wick Poetry Chapbook
Contest at Kent State University Press and are reprinted by permission of Kent State University Press.

Special thanks to The Milton Center in Wichita, Kansas, who offered me the 1997-98 Milton Center
Writing Fellowship to complete this project, and to the Ludwig Vogelstein Foundation for a timely grant.

Book design: Elaine LaMattina

Printed and bound in the United States of America.

White Pine Press, P.O. Box 236, Buffalo, NY 14201.

Image on page 7: "Self Portrait Drawing at a Window," 1648. Rembrandt Harmenszoon van Rijn, Dutch,
1606-1669. Etching and drypoint on paper, 158 x 129 mm. (sheet), Robert Forsythe Collection,
1924.1731. Photograph ©2001, The Art Institute of Chicago. All Rights Reserved.

Library of Congress Cataloging-in-Publication Data

Frech, Stephen, 1969–

   If not for these wrinkles of darkness : Rembrandt a self portrait / Stephen Frech

p.   cm.

ISBN 1-893996-13-1 (pbk. : alk. paper)

1. Rembrandt Harmenszoon van Rijn, 1606-1669–Poetry. 2. Netherlands–Poetry.
3. Painting–Poetry. 4. Painters–Poetry. I. Title

PS3556 R3655 I38 2001

811'.54–dc21   2001023541

                                            CIP

Again, for Annalyse, my first

and

for Amelio Barbaro, in memory of Cecilia Cox Barbaro

Als ik mijn geest uitspanning wil geven, dan is het
niet eer die ik zoek, maar vrijheit.

When I give greater latitude to my spirit,
I seek not honor but freedom.

—Rembrandt van Rijn
(as quoted by Arnold Houbraken, 1718)

CONTENTS

I

Endure a Little / 11
The Windmill / 13
Who Lives Alone Longs for Mercy / 15
Descent from the Cross / 16
Spring Gathers in the Ground Below Me / 17
Letter to Jan Lievens, 1633 / 19
Female Nude of a Woman I've Never Seen Naked / 21
Simeon in the Temple / 22
Rhyme for the Procuress in Springtime / 23
Christ at Emmaus / 24

II

Respice in Faciem Christi / 25
The Green Crawler Finds its Way / 27
Rembrandt in the Studio with Pupils / 28
Self-Portrait with Saskia: The Prodigal Son in the Tavern / 29
Chiaroscuro / 31
Cornelia II / 32
Sketches Toward the Flight into Egypt / 33
Letter to Cornelis Anslo, 1641 / 37
I'm Cross with God Who Has Wrecked this Generation / 38
Who'd Have Thought the Owl so Fierce? / 39

III

My Leman on the Road / 41
Letter to Carel Fabritius, September 1643 / 43
The Adoration of the Shepherds / 44
The Hog / 45
Song for Titus When He Asks for a Second Dessert / 46
Bird Cries from the Nest in the Eaves
    at Morning: Self-Portrait / 47
Hendrickje Stoffels / 48
Crows, Just Before Flight / 49
Awake at Night Ruined by the Mocking / 50

IV

I Would Be Clad in Christ's Skin / 51

Woman Bathing / 53

The Bricklayer's Sled / 54

Letter to Carel Fabritius, October 1654 / 56

The Denial of Peter / 58

Prayer for the Maker / 59

To Live this Close to Deer / 60

Farmhouses that at Anchor Seemed / 61

Return of the Lost Son / 63

Chronology / 65

I.

Endure a Little

Lord, you called to me
like gulls to shipwrecked sailors long at sea:
"endure yet!" "endure a little!"
But, adrift and wave-weary,
I answered, oh, dreadfully:
"yet" and "yet" is endless
and "endure a little" is a long way.

The Windmill

To have ears for immaterial things:
the incoming whisper of wings cutting the air,
the groan of children's bones growing,
the quiet after thunder when planks in the floor,
shingles, lattice, everything has a breath
and you can hear it.
I had to strain beyond the cooing of mourning doves.
I had to crawl. My father ordered,
so I crawled into the tight dark behind the grind-stone.
Pot-bellied like a barrel,
stable as a gourd upright on a table,
my father's mill had no corners.
In the back, no dust stirred.
Every barley corn had to be salvaged,
but, afraid of what my hand might find
searching, I settled for one handful.
I had no eyes for the dark then,
and with the floors shaking, my ears full
of the rumble of the great stone turning,
I lost myself.
My father had to drag me out by my ankles.
I emerged, upside down in my father's powerful grip
like a sack shaken for its last few kernels,
wet-faced with a fist of grain.

Gusts begin to swirl and the miller
turns the blades, locks them in irons,
rolls their canvases, and disengages the transfer.
The stones settle into each other
while the storm outside breaks
on the prow of the miller's shack.
The backdoor of the mill bangs in its jam

as if someone leaves repeatedly in anger.
The day clouds; the dust in the mill rises.
Stumbling in just such a dusty dark,
we could have our noses to the wall
and stupidly not know it. Or we could sweep our hands
around us for some fixture we think
is barely out of reach, when really we're in
some vast space.
We fumble in the dark like a thief
who snuffed his light at the slightest sound—
it was his own shoe shuffle—and now
can't find his way. He will have
what he came for, though, so he grabs
a sack of he knows not what
and scrambles for the sound of wind
whistling through a crack.
The sack is light—he figures, once in the street,
he can run with it.

Who Lives Alone Longs for Mercy

I saw three thugs beating another man on the road
in the not-yet-dark when everything is gray.
One drove his heel into the fallen man's open hand.
A second twisted a leg unnaturally far to restrain him.
The third, kneeling on the chest, pounded his fists
against the victim's face. Snot and blood spattered
the chin of the beaten man.

The heavy weave of the assaulter's coat;
the fabric bunched where a snag had been repaired;
the rose that flushed his face with exertion;
the grunts that invested in each blow—
I noted that his hat didn't fit,
that it never fell from his head.
But my cry wouldn't out; my legs wouldn't run.
I was afraid of the boot-soles of grown men,
of a heavy forearm pinning my head to the ground.
Who knew what they were doing?
Who knew what they wanted?
Any shift in the night air might signal them
to look and find me there, witness to their mean party.
And they had one to spare and one was more than enough
for me—I was thirteen.
I just stood and held my holler deep in my throat.
The dog that was with them, so used to the scene
and cruelty that he didn't bark,
looked up in my direction, stared right at me,
and watched me as I, alone, thirteen,
silently watched the whole thing.

Descent from the Cross

Had he been a sack of grain, the fullness
would not have buckled like this man,
purely flesh. Death does not inhabit
the body; it leaves it without intent,

leaves it cumbersome and unwieldy,
and there's no easy way to carry a dead man.
The workmen were shamed by their clumsiness,
his nudity and the body's lack of humility.

The workman's cheek burned as it braced
against the cooling abdomen
and, while they worked to free him,
a sweet, salty musk rose from his loins,

invaded the workman's nostrils
and he blushed to be so close, to feel
the last warmth leaving the body,
and to know, finally, it all passes

so quietly and into the dirt.
If it weren't for the torchlight, they would look
like robbers in a neighbor's orchard,
ladders leaned to the ghastly trees,

gathering bushels and bagsful of fruit.

Spring Gathers in the Ground Below Me

Dr. Tulp's class crowds the corpse.
Hand flexion: carpi radialus, ulnaris,
digitorum, palmaris. The flexors in the forearm
slip through sheaths banded at the wrist.
The dead hand mimics the living that manipulates it,
only the dead man grabs at nothing.

The butcher's hands tire of the cleaver.
The callused hands of my father no longer blistered.
My mother's hand followed text as she read.
The foreigner's hand points as he utters the word for "tree"
in another language. The tree stays in its place
in both languages.

How I hold the brush came to me without study,
but that my hand at work so close to the wet canvas
could never ground itself or brace there
was an ache my shoulder had to learn.
And growing accustomed to that pain
and its trembling assures nothing.

The hand's work lurks in subterranean string-tugging,
the restlessness of the body's larger tissue.
Our limitless wanderings begin
in the pure mechanics of the hand, fashioning ships,
shepherding them to uncharted waters,
and pointing to unknown beaches.
Cartographers pen the shoreline,
their fingers black with ink.
In the margins, native flora rise
as they do every spring in remote meadows.

The most simple gestures startle the earth:
a bean seed nudging aside the dirt clods,

straightening, stiff, new-green.
Pale pink blossoms, delicate, finely drawn—
surely these are the plant's object.
But when the first strong wind scatters the blossoms
is the vine spent?
No—the new-green darkens yet and broods
the pods that take weeks to fill and stretch.
Spring gathers in the ground below me, teeming,
and the blunt end of my brush uncovers it.

Letter to Jan Lievens, 1633

Bulbs sprout in the barrel on long journeys—
packed tight in the dark must seem like earth.
But the barrel is not the earth,
and the sprouting pales.
In the market, workmen pry the lids open
and the barrels look like so many bulbs teeming with asps.
The gardeners wizard them into the ground,
so the fields, with tulip stems,
open like a lady's fan.

Blue cups a hand to its mouth to call out:
the metallic blue of certain cuts of meat,
the angry blue of jays,
blue beetles, bells, Delft china,
clean current blue that is not really blue,
but the shrimp that follow it.
Reds lust, and part the curtains.
Yellow mimics the sun:
young-leaf yellow, autumn decay,
the golden crust of cross-buns,
grain left in the field to dry,
a bruise healing,
honey, amber, the jaundiced eye.

We're eclipsed by fields of our own making.
The lush fields exceed my palette;
my Saskia exceeds the fields.
You and I, we dreamed of goddesses, peerless women
we will never lose because we'll never gain.
Extremes of beauty terrified us
as chimera of hopeless longings,
but we were wrong to think of beauty
as those things we'll never have.
If we're consumed by objects of our desire,

perhaps we should let ourselves be taken.

Perfect sun. Good earth.
Failures at the canvas. Fathomless.
Seamless vessel. Did I mention berries earlier?
Like none other, each of them.
Saskia—object and lesson—is bright,
upright as the tulips, delicate as petals.
These flowers and Saskia—Amsterdam is rich,
my friend: commissions and beauty and light.

Female Nude of a Woman I've Never Seen Naked

We've missed the point perhaps in making something beautiful.
We admire those things most that meet their purpose:
a stream of ants, the flower of eggplant,
the fine cut of a spinnaker filled in a strong wind.
But what should we make of our bodies,
all this flesh and its various turnings:
blemishes flaring, hairs cropping up?
Pride blinds us to our own ugliness, that skin
under the arm that begins to wrinkle, then wilt.
We wear ourselves dry and thick where we were once soft,
fingertips callused from working the washboard,
nipples tired from nursing the brood.

Undress simply, as if you were alone.
The garter and corset straps leave their impressions;
let your belly hang bottom-heavy as a pear,
pleased to sag and be as unshapely as it wishes,
every stretch of you tired, loose, fleshy,
but easeful and relaxed as in a warm bath
and inviting me to stare.
Now, imagine someone loving you for all that.

Simeon in the Temple

She hated to give him up,
but the old man was so insistent
she passed Jesus into his arms
and for a moment it was just the two,

Simeon and the infant white as knuckles
of a fist. He could not be mistaken:
here was the one who had sustained him
that to hold him at last ...
It stole his breath.
Dying entered him,
the very moment ripe apples are picked,
so he returned the child to Mary and said:

Yea, a sword shall pierce thy own soul also,
slash the horizon, and create a slit
for the sun to slip through.

Rhyme for the Procuress in Springtime

The first spring rain cools a cup of tea too hot to drink.
You follow the rain's falling until you think
its angle is true plumb and the world must have tilted
while you looked away to pick your thumbnail until it bled.

The humid air smells of young women working and damp wood.
How should the deep-grooved bark of lindens like the comparison?
How about the woodpecker busy there for mites? The squirrel?
The pearl of sunlight on the apple's skin?

Who will cut the apple slices thin?
Who will take the mad dog in?
Who will stretch the damp cloth?
Who investigate screams from the bog?

The rain comes down, the rain comes down.
Lift your skirts, ladies—the canal's at the door
lapping for your babies.

Christ at Emmaus

One asked the stranger to divide the bread
and the flame wavered as if a breeze crept in.
Pausing for a moment, the inn's day done,
he listened to the distant kitchen clatter,
a woman bent over a basin
scrubbing one day's grime from new pots—
tomorrow, who can discern yesterday's from today's?

So the stranger took the loaf in both hands,
measured with his thumbs the seam
where he intended to break it,
showed it to one man saying, "This is for you."
As the crust tore, the cup tipped
and spilled its wine that ran the length
and seeped through the cracks of the table's planks.

Knowing him at last, am I the one frozen in surprise
or the other, fallen to my knees, my eyes cast down
seeing some far field I've never lost sight of
and that, if only I'd set out, a day's walking
would have brought to me.

II.

Respice in Faciem Christi

Look to the Lord, Man, hanging on the tree,
and weep for all that blood shed for you and for me.
Thorns fasten the vine wound round his head;
the spear to prick his life away opened another wound instead.
His fair face fades.
His sight grows dim.
His body, naked, glistening with sweet blood from every side
sags against the nails, stiffening his arms stretched wide.
Begin at his head and look to his toe:
no salve, nothing to save us but anguish and woe.

The Green Crawler Finds its Way

Mint sends out shoots, blind worms that crawl
along the surface. The plant survives not by prudence,
but wantonness, abandon: tendrils creep
in all directions, drop fine roots blindly,
not because the ground is good, but out of habit
every few inches, a living yardstick of regularity.
If they take, they take. The plant moves on.
Left to its own devices, mint will devour the garden.
Having found a low spot where the bricks have settled,
a shoot will crawl through the constant damp,
across a road or path to another garden patch.

The love of mint, then, is not limited to taste,
but includes the constant clipping and a large bite
of the spade through a crowd of tangled roots.
The art of holding back always fuels the possibility—
you have only to stop resisting—of wildness, green and lush.
In the tavern, under the table, a hand touches
the heavy part of the thigh and is pushed away.
Next week, she'll wait for you to take
such liberties and you anticipate the reproach,
until it becomes a lovely exchange:
May I please?   *No you may not.*
May I please?   *No, we shouldn't.*
And the mint in the garden,
even with your close attention,
grabs hold of the rosemary
and swallows the thyme.

Rembrandt in the Studio with Pupils

How do muscles carry us,
lift us from the ground with nothing above,
no pulley or boom to grab hold and raise us?
Our muscles, every twitching fiber,
taut tendon, and placement on the bone
ally against the ground like stalks of hyacinths:
one great effort to blossom, sure, relentless.

You have forgotten how to walk like a child.
You have forgotten your own evolution.
Down on the floor, all of you. Down
flat with your faces against the boards.
Now lift yourselves, stand up.
That other body that slides beneath
the skin, it knows only one way of painting,
but the only painting you will ever be good at.

Self-Portrait with Saskia:
       The Prodigal Son in the Tavern

Why reduce myself to rags,
my rags of clothing to a last patch of modesty?

Frayed by the dog who tore at my sleeve,
confused by the first worn and tired vision
I saw of myself in a pool,
even picking gravel from under the skin of my knees,
I would still remember the coins
jangling in my purse, the price
good tobacco commands, and the cloud of it
whorling in my lungs and in my head.

Why must I paint myself as the Prodigal Son
returned shabby and repentant?
Even reduced to eating swine-meal,
having to kick the snouts away,
I would still relish in what passes my lips,
hunger for more than what I have.
Repentance, then, is bad fortune, hardship,
and longing.

I fatten my dry lip to split it,
hold the sweet tobacco on that crack.
The leaf burns at first, but eases me into numbness.
I smolder with the pipe and everything I've held
just so in my teeth: jeweled scimitars,
draw-strings, cork stoppers, lacing, nipples.

I've painted myself in the tavern with a woman
who lets me touch her and a glass of wine
so tall, it exceeds the length of my arm
from elbow to finger-tip.
I'll ignore the lightness of it all and the winds

picking up—I know how this story ends
and the good father will forgive me.

Chiaroscuro

Saskia, from where do shadows come?
The sundial's restless one, cast
as if by an arrow just landed, still trembling,
darkens the day hour by hour.

Shadows long as avenues
greet us at every corner.
Our own shadow touches us
at the soles of our feet.
Dark surrounds us endlessly,
enduring even daylight.

Are these shades pieces of black?
Is the dark broken
or is it a thing of many parts
that needs to be put together?

To paint by candlelight or lamp
highlights every mound of you,
shadows every fold and crease;
each breast nurses one of twin crescent shades.
Light unveils a darkness my body longs for.
In the background lurks the dark
that a wavering flame barely holds at bay.

Your skin is as good as wax, pricey, pure,
with a consistency even the sweetest cream lacks.
You own shadows and give them to me
as gifts. And only when you are spent
will darkness truly come for me.

Cornelia II

I can hardly lift her, the third and only child,
to my lips. Slight as she is, she's too much for me.
We've filled her with more than we can carry—
too much slops over the brim, runs down,

and wets our grip. Why torment me
with vinegar when I've asked for wine?
Why drip it on my tongue, dry out my mouth,
and always leave me thirsty and bitter?

We've been clipped back severely
and will turn a season without fruit.
We will be the one tree in the orchard
good only for shade, a place to lean tools,

to hang damp shirts of workmen at noon to dry.
First Rombartus, then Cornelia,...
Saskia, this one who won't make it,
what should I name her?

Sketches Toward The Flight into Egypt

i.
The midday sun buckled the bridge boards
with a heat like breath from the bellows.
After a rainless month, it burned the grass
it had once stirred.
The wildflowers' pollen crackled in the heat;
the flames claimed an acre of wheat.
The rest of the harvest, ground into flour,
baked into bread, had a smoky taste.
Goats, knowing full well that grass returns,
step slowly into the spent field,
raise then plant one foot at a time,
each hoof stirring a cloud of ash
that dusts their ankles.

ii.
They woke at night and walked for hours
when it was cool. Joseph rose and lit a lamp
that without the moon lumined
only a small section of the road,
barely visible side to side.
When Mary stirred, the landscape she'd seen
was gone: the hills far off,
the tall reeds that marked the creek.
The world she'd wakened to seemed smaller
than the one that had lulled her to sleep
and she debated till dawn whether this
was a comfort or a fright.

iii.
Beyond the light you do not know;
you do not know the road ahead,
where the road turns or when,
if the road unrolls like fabric

from the bolt in front and, if so,
if the road rolls up again behind.
Joseph leads the beast;
Mary, riding, nodding off to sleep
to the clop, clop, clop of the donkey's feet,
dreams of brick after brick set in its place
and a wall rising up or a legion of soldiers
marching on the stone roads.

iv.
Cattle gather roadside, lowing.
Sheep have flooded the road like white sea foam.
The travelers wade through the bleating.
A crow flies overhead: There are three. There are three.
The sheep, too low, can't see
and leap one over another.
The cows pull up grass with their teeth;
a calf hurries beside his mother,
nudges the teat trying to feed.
The donkey nods through:
burden, sweet burden.

v.
Mary hums a little; Joseph broods
while his fingers worry a stone smooth
deep in his pocket. The new night
reddens at the setting.
The child emerges like citrus from the rind:
plump, bright-eyed, clean even without washing,
learning from Mary the need of holding onto things—
a lesson to be learned for this world,
a lesson to be unlearned at its departing.

vi.

The child dozes and wakes, so new
how can he know which is the world
and which the dream? Which is the fold of fabric,
the hills fallen to valleys, the deep furrows of bark?
On the road, he lived like kittens in a sack,
deep in his mother's clothing, swaddled in a wrap.
He knew already the mother's scent:
salt and coriander, mild cheese,
an alfalfa field after rain;
a world of thin, sweet milk, the warm breast,
and the delicious sweat that runs between them.

vii. *Returned, I Lay Down with Saskia and the Paintings*

If I had all the paint and skill,
I'd sketch the whole road leading home,
mark it as with piles of stones.
With the landscape painted,
we could walk for miles
and not worry of losing our way
or wonder how far we've traveled,
how much farther we have to go.
This is the tree where I held you first.
This is the bush where we ate.
This is the cross-road we'll never take,
this the route we'll have to return by.
Here we stopped once and crawled
into the wheat field, matted down the grass
like deer at night, tried to keep quiet
though the breath had to come,
and the stalks that still stood and touched us,
their grain quivered at the tip.
This one marks where you will tire,

send me on ahead and I will continue
strangely happy somehow,
knowing where you are and how to get there.

Letter to Cornelis Anslo, 1641

You are right—the likeness of your wife
is not entirely faithful. But I have composed her
with the deepest reverence that no one body
can contain. So why not the hands
of a woman used to kneading?
Why not the keen eyes of a seamstress?
The forehead of high intelligence?
Sometimes, walking home after listening
to the fine embroidery of your voice,
I feel not myself or as if I've outgrown
the suit of my own skin.
We clip the wick that burns the candle
too quickly—you see, simple and true exceed
the thing itself and the one who speaks it,
be he painter or preacher.
We're more than we'll ever know.
You ask me a question I can't answer.
I will say instead that a bird
flying high above the ground
can see through shallow lakes to their beds,
the sunken log, the fish that gather,
the line and lure that miss them.

I'm Cross with God Who Has Wrecked This Generation

The son survives; my wife died,
withered slowly, a whisper of herself in bed.
Left alone, I eat my crust everyday without wine.
Times I try to soothe away the baby's cries—
so much wailing the ears can only take—
these hands, clumsy mitts,
her sure gestures poorly mimic.
This one's mine and I have nothing
to offer this simplest of creatures.

I will waste away, poor
and grown bitter with sadness long endured.
An apple fallen to the ground sweetens at the bruise.
But days later, who can bear the stink
sweltering in the grass, the bees
crawling around in the muck?

What cruel mercy stole my wife?
You sent your bastard son wandering
in search of a father. Why must we?
Like some god-damned leeshore,
you have every intent to wreck me.
How, broken then on the rocks, am I
to ask you for peace and mercy?
You think you found a new way of gathering
fruit from high branches, but how short-sighted
is banging the apple tree?

Who'd Have Thought the Owl So Fierce?

At night, when the whole flock herds together,
each shoving her way to the warm center,
the sound of stronger wings descends.
There's commotion in the flock—the talons
of a great horned owl select the tired or the weak,
sink the claws in deep, lance the life
with a hold that won't lose her in flight.
Those nearest the victim cry out a defense.
When the chicken is lifted away,
the others quiet down, return to their low sounds
and shoving. I sleep soundly; the dog
has merely raised his head.

I sleep through the night without you now,
but these dreams, when I remember them,
frighten me. The days are plain.
Our son, who continues to grow, starts from his sleep,
a crying from which there's no soothing.
But these, you'd be happy to know,
grow more and more infrequent.

III.

My Leman on the Road

When I see by the road,
   nailed fast to the tree,
   Jesus my beloved, heaven-bound,
beaten black and bloody,
beside him Mother Mary, Saint John,

His body bitten by the scourge,
his side deeply stung
   for the guilt of men
   and the ghosts to raise up,
quickly I fall to weeping,
give the tears to my hands,
fall to weeping,
if only I can,
if only I can.

Letter to Carel Fabritius, September 1643

I groan when I think of you in that low spot
where the fields dip like a shallow bowl
and your house lists on piles driven
into the deepest pool of a drained lake.

As if the winds have failed you,
the mill blades cast a steady shadow,
and the pumps gurgled and stopped,
death has swamped your house again:

the one baby, then your wife.
And now I hear the second child, Catrina, has died.
Oh, Carel, your loss winters the night.

The Adoration of the Shepherds

They entered slowly like birds wanting bread.
Unlike any other seed they know,
it stirs a hunger a day of feeding won't sate,
a longing so desperate that, skittish, with quick eyes
watchful for the other fist,
they risk feeding from your hand.

The smell of the barn fouled the nostrils:
the day had been long and hot,
the animals labored hard.
Crushed bindweed dried on the hooves of cattle;
the horse's collar hung on the wall,
its padded leather still damp and ripe with horse brine.
And hay, just on the far side of fermenting,
spiked the air and kept the cows dreamy and docile.

An old man carries a dim lamp into the light of the barn
and the flame is merely flame now—a busy sliver.
It hardly casts shadows of its own;
its light barely reaches the rotting loft boards.

He hadn't expected this, not at all:
a new mother, so young and at ease
with the baby as only young mothers can be,
generous with all the strangers craning to take a look.
She doesn't know—how could she?
The shadow on her breast is only of her hand.

The Hog

Tired by the sheer size of himself,
mountainous, rough, the hog dropped
across the doorway, hoof-bound, footsore,
docile now from the struggle that sweetens meat.

The children poked him with sticks
to see if he was spent. When even a snort
was too much for him, the children crept closer
to touch with one finger, a whole hand,
and then, emboldened by their risk, the hot,
foul smell of his skin, to stand on this tired lump.
His breathing raised them, then dropped them.
Twenty minutes at least before the beast recovers
and, by then, the father will have opened
one of its veins.

With the hog drawn, hung-up, and draining,
the father opens the belly with a heavy cleaver
and, among the warm sacks and globes, his hand
finds the bladder and cuts it out.
He drains it, passes it to his children
who will blow it up and tie both ends
or fill it with chrysanthemum water.
The juice will taste that much sweeter
because they know where the sack came from
and it was promised to them
when they and the hog were about the same size.

Song for Titus When He Asks for a Second Dessert

Toward something sweet the berry grows
hard at first as a stone and green,
emerging wrinkled, naked as possum pups,
pale as the skin of just shorn sheep.

Sun and steady rain fuel the fruit;
even the moon loves a berry underripe
and coaxes the sugared out of her skirt
of green leaves, darkening like the night.

We're tied to blackberries grown wild in the wood,
bound to the fruit still gripping the bush,
attached to those fallen that stain the grass,
delighted captives to the last.

Bird Cries from the Nest in the Eaves at Morning: Self-Portrait

When the mother's gone the young sparrows cry.
They cry not knowing for what: hunger,
cold, fear that mother will not return?
So, when the sun is not yet up
and barn swallows are busy swooping
around the knees of horses and cattle
wandered out to pasture, the young sparrows
cry from their nest, cry together
not knowing that the cat is on his hind-legs
pawing for them, cry together heard by
they don't know what, watched by me at my window,
happy to hear them, annoyed at having been wakened,
calculating the progress of the cat's claw.

Hendrickje Stoffels

I have stolen the gesture of your arms
at that moment of opening your body
as if it were a baker's cabinet—
warm, damp from the breads and pies cooling.

Old habits are harder to break than bone.
I nap on the studio floor
though I can feel every crack, every cold day endured
in the crown of my bones
bearing my weight against the wood.
You haven't said a chiding word.
Instead, the smell of your zucchini bread I love
fills the house and wakes me.
You work long hours,
your forearms dusted with flour,
your hands smeared with butter.
I am impatient with the oven and the long wait.

Then you, suddenly, at my door,
having skipped the third step that creaks—
why wait so long after knocking?
The door is open—step in and be my wife.

Crows, Just Before Flight

The flock exceeds the tree—
this seemed important to say before I said it.
Or that the elm tree, bough laden,
lush with crows, groans in a light breeze,
croons with the throat-purr, coos, and wing flutter.
The crows fold darkness around them
like another set of wings that borrows the moonlight
and lacquers the tree crown.

The flock exceeds the tree and still
crows gather, waiting—any moment
like a spark introduced to black powder
they'll break from their dark
and their bodies will fragment the sky like flaws in glass.

I held a jar once, just filled with hot cabbage,
above my head to see what I had made
and to feel the cool glass warm as the soup settled.
In an instant, the jar cracked but didn't shatter—
the whole vessel shook as if something inside it
had been struck by a hammer and made a sound.
Terrific to have a warming thing,
broken in your hands, remain whole.

Nothing likens that feeling and only etching
can crack the sky and repair it in the same plate:
crosshatched cloud banks, the rain's insistent angle falling.
The burin's furrow trails the plow and opens the ground.
A farmer stands in his open field in seed-time;
three trees are left on a slope the team can't handle.
All of this seemed important to say before I said it.

Awake at Night, Ruined by the Mocking

A cockroach crawled across my chest last night
and to feel another living thing in bed besides my wife
started me like the fright of one bird that stirs
the whole feeding flock to wing, a banked cloud rising.

His legs tangled in the hair, a delicate touch,
a struggle the pit of me remembered,
but I didn't move; I hardly even stiffened.
I was ashamed to be found naked in bed,
shamed to be found at all in the poverty of my own flesh,
without a nightshirt, in a borrowed bed,
a house that's not my own.

The warm chest and beating heart hurried him
and I let him cross, too afraid to touch him
and to waken Hendrickje to my disgrace.

Then, when his hard body knocked against the floor,
I lept from the bed, grabbed the large basin
from the stand and trapped him beneath it
in the middle of the room.
I returned to bed and tucked myself in tight.
I didn't kill him till morning so all night
he dragged the hard shell of him round and round the rim
and the large basin hummed like a bell.

IV.

I Would Be Clad in Christ's Skin

I will find there rich, nourishing food—
a modest feast that more than all the bowls
and flagons hold will free me from this hunger,
wash from my tongue the thirst for this world's wine.
I would be clad in Christ's skin,
that ran with streams of blood he lost,
that let his whole heart out to let mine in.

Woman Bathing

Freed from shelling peas and shucking oysters
from their salt-pearled shells,
your hands find the hem of your slip
and gather the fabric's length up to your thighs.

A stranger might think you meant to carry
fruit and had forgotten your bucket.
But you raise your slip above the river's glass
and pause in the current:

your neckline low, hem held high,
the arms that raise it, the thighs striding there.
Gold, amber, evening shades of blue enter you
and haunt the cloth.

Can you see the birds gathering in your skin?
They're hungry, bone-tired
from constantly breaking a space open
for themselves in the air.

And still the white shines through,
brilliant and rare like the coconut's white.
That you step from the bank
into a stream you don't know,

feel with one foot the uneven, descending bed
and find a firm spot, unseen, to bear your weight
sustains me like winter gardens
and wild raspberries late in the season.

To find you in my life's dark thicket ...
Hold that Hendrickje; don't move—just as you are
is all I've wanted, all I'll ever need.

The Bricklayer's Sled

Snow eases the horse's burden of bricks
on low-sled runners Willem slicks with a lump
of salvaged candle drippings.
So the old horse on winter roads hauls the load
as he once did.

After days of deep freeze, Willem and I
unload the yard of brick and ride the sled
to the harbor. Skating honeys the day
for toddlers and their nurses, for the school children,
boys who frisk like spring ponies
and practice tricks in front of the girls holding hands.
Willem and I race back and forth across the ice
hauling a line of boys until they gain
too much speed, crash, and slide in a pile.

Tavern owners push their carts to the dock
to sell warmed cider and glühwein.
Willem and I down a few tankards quick
and I notice for the first time the knuckle
he's opened to the bone that morning—
he laughs and clenches his hand into a fist to show me.

By afternoon, I'm drunk and we're racing faster.
My arms strain to reach around his broad shoulders
and my belly between us. All the skaters we pass so quickly
look like stuffed dolls in their winter wear.
And for the day on the ice we laugh like young men,
still newly-married to our first wives ...
no, like boys who have fooled our masters
and stolen away from work.

The steady clop of the horse's hooves
and their echoes through the ice,
the call of nurses, the hoots of boys,
all drown our laughing and calls to the horse for more speed.
In my arms I can feel Willem's body shake
and the warmth coming off him
as if he were sobbing.
Only when he throws his head back
on my shoulder can I hear his laugh
so close it dampens my ear.

Letter to Carel Fabritius, October 1654

Butcher, baker, silversmith,
cobbler, miller, carpenter, painter:
we all walked to our masters as boys
frightened and slack-shouldered,
never to wield the other's ballpeen,
maulstick, or plane.

But you came to me a carpenter, a fabritius,
carrying in your muscled torso
knowledge of the roof's pitch and the eave's protection.

Most of what I knew I could teach you
because it was learned. But you, my dear Carel,
will have to continue selling: your knowledge
slept deep in those arms I've seen
sink a nail in two strokes;
yours is a gift you cannot pass on or give away.

I saw your *Goldfinch* and in the bird's throat
wavered the beginning notes of a song
I have sung only under my wings
and thought nobody heard. Your goldfinch
looked about to call it to the crowded room,
recite it word for word—my song, only harped
on a better instrument, played by more skillful hands.

Even after the goldfinch resigns
to the perch and the hinged feedbox,
when he wakes, he must forget sometimes
and seeing no bars think he's free:
the shadow he casts on the wall
out-measures the chain that holds him there;
his song fills the kitchen, rises above
the sound of cloves being ground in the mortar,

higher than the hook that waits
for the achilles tendon of the lamb's leg.
Like waves against a breaker, the tethered
dash themselves to the chain's limit.
I want to hold the goldfinch's chain in my hand
to feel the urgent tug his wings could muster.

I stared away an hour with the painting
and the bird's onyx eye outlasted me—I'm burdened
with blinking, with eyes that dry and blur.
You and I and the bird: we were whole once.
Maybe we were there together.

The Denial of Peter

This was your true calling, Peter,
the echo in the wood, the voice from shore.
There is no other wilderness but here:
brier of swords, tangle of accusation.

I know him not.

Her hand cups the candle's flame;
she has seen you with him.
Chiaroscuro of discovery, suggestion,
light and line of vision all point to you.

I know not what thou sayest.

Christ looks over his shoulder
and this gaze alone could melt you
like mushrooms too long in sight of the sun.
You have just turned back from him,

your hand still warms from his cheek
and now as his image floats above your palm ...
Oh Peter, you know the moment you open
your mouth you will lie.

I do not know the man.

Prayer for the Maker

Given leaves, could we reconstruct the tree?
Given a nest, could we cite the bird that wove it,
the fabric that used the thread she stole?
It's too late to ask the worm she ate,
though he probably knows.

How can we know the potter from the bowl he threw;
the miller from the sack of ground wheat;
the fisherman from the nets he stitched,
the hooks he bent, the barbs cut?

Could we study the young and know their parents?
If it's true the object never exceeds the maker,
then how do we keep from descending?
What hope is there for children? for the object made?
for the maker who suffers the sight of it?

Without the fine details, our lives suffer.
We seek them out, yet they bring to mind
the slackness of skin at morning
and the trembling at dusk—
and so, with fine details, we suffer.

Lord, today I put my finger in a friend's mouth
to feel the edge of a tooth just chipped
and wondered how the tongue moves unscathed in there.

To Live this Close to Deer

Deer shy to the woods at daybreak,
follow their long shadows back,
careful to place their hooves going out
in the prints they left in the clearing coming in.
Their strides quicken near the woods
as if the open field itself took aim,
steadied a drawn bowstring
and were about to release it.
Still, they turn sometimes, just in the brush,
to see us looking after them.

Musk lingers in the fog of early morning—
deer have been walking the edges of the city
like lone animals after the plague, this time,
has claimed everyone.

Drawn by the smells of grain and vegetables
stored in bins outside the kitchen door,
they navigate the arched alleyway,
suffer the clicks of their hooves on bricks and tile,
nudge the gate, and enter the courtyard.

I've heard that one, startled, will bash himself
nearly to death in a cramped space
before he discovers the way he entered.
I've never found one at my door.
Many times, though, having thought I was alone,
I found winged hoof prints in the mud,
so fresh they're still filling with ground water.

Farmhouses that at Anchor Seemed

The leaves that chased me never won,
but at this pace, I can't catch the hare
who rests now in the moon.

To stop and untangle a cluster of burrs from my trousers
is a task I love—I have been out walking
and seen a piece of paper wrapped around a branch
by the river's current. How long until the sodden paper tears?

The hooks of the burrs are set and holding.

That the paper chose the tree
or the tree plucked the paper from the river's breeze
doesn't matter now that the branch
wears it like a skin.

And the tree that chose me, I won't let go.
Though the branch is stronger than I expected,
if the current's going to take me,
the branch will have to break.

Long ago, I thought my bones would betray me.
Brittle sticks, how could they hold the raw muscle of me?

Wolves never think of their bones or that long ago
wolves abandoned stealth. The pack hunts together
and the hip joints slide in their casings
without the wolves wishing it so, or ever doubting it,
and when a bone shard pricks the soft tissue,
he withers quickly while the pack flourishes
within sight, but beyond him.
He watches them crest each hill
farther and farther away.
When the echo of my last footfall has faded,

will people strain to hear if truly it has passed away?

The whale who threw himself on the beach
lived for days rasping in at the blow hole, sighing out.
Women walked to the shore twice a day with buckets
for their share of oil, but the men leaned on their lances,
waiting—still the whale gasped.
I fought the urge to chalk him in my sketchpad
and visited no longer when his loins let go
and wouldn't stop growing, colossal, larger than a man,
not erect, but the full length extended,
flaccid, all of him lay on the beach coated in sand.

On hot days I was hardly more than animal,
thirsting. A snake drinks and will drown
in a saucer of milk, fat in the middle,
kneading the slow body-grip of a mouse swallowed whole.

Oh, even the cactus leans toward the sun.

My knocking against the trunk in high winds soured my juice.
My place on the tree determined the color of my rind.

The plow's eight inch bite of earth
is a shallow taste, but the most delicious,
turning each furrow to a loaf.
But to plow the field is also an undoing —
voles have been turned out of their burrows;
both halves of the cut worm wriggle for holes;
crows in their black robes land in the field.

And the press that takes the print also wears the plate down.

Return of the Lost Son

It is color that carries our lives
out of shadow, all the flesh-tones
in a peach. We should learn to handle
each other in this way, like fresh fruit,

like something meant to be beautiful
and nourishing. The father lays his hands on
with this gentleness. He embraces shadows
in the son's clothes. If it were not

for these wrinkles of darkness,
his hands would be lost.
This is the back he knew, the one
that grew and spread in the fields,

like oregano in the garden, thinner now,
every bone countable, but accounted for.
His hands cannot hold the way
he wants them to. When his son, an infant,

slept in his arms even then
his hands were not enough
to hold him with all the joy and ochre
that emerge from shadows,

the golden grip of sunflowers.

Chronology

1606, July 15:   Rembrandt van Rijn is born in Leiden, son of a miller and a baker's daughter, the eighth of nine children.

1623   Rembrandt studies in Amsterdam for six months under the eminent historical painter Pieter Lastman, admirer of Caravaggio and his technique of chiaroscuro.

1624   Rembrandt returns to Leiden and sets himself up as an independent master, developing a close friendship and working relationship with artist Jan Lievens.

1625   Rembrandt's first known painting, *The Stoning of St. Stephen*, includes the first of his many self-portraits: his face is among the crowd of murderers.

1631-32   Rembrandt moves to Amsterdam.

1632   Rembrandt paints *The Anatomy Lesson of Dr. Tulp*, his first considerable commission. The painting's dramatic and pyramidal composition coupled with the stunning skill of its individual portraits make Rembrandt an instant success and the '30s his most productive and lucrative decade.

1633   A sketch of Saskia with the words:
"This is drawn after my wife when she was 21 years old, the third day after our betrothal—the 8th June, 1633."

1635   Rembrandt's first child, Rombartus born; dies at two months

1638   Rembrandt's second child, Cornelia born; dies in infancy

1639   Rembrandt purchases, with heavy mortgage, a beautiful house on St. Anthoniesbreestraat in the Jewish quarter of Amsterdam.

1640   Rembrandt's third child, Cornelia II born; dies in infancy

1641-1643   Carel Fabritius studies in Rembrandt's studio. He will go on to be Rembrandt's most accomplished student, even believed to have functioned briefly as one of Vermeer's instructors. He will die on October 12, 1654, when his wall collapses on him as result of an accidental explosion in Delft's town arsenal.

1641, September   Rembrandt and Saskia's fourth child, a son, Titus is born.

1642, June	Saskia dies after a long illness resulting from pregnancy and birth complications.
1649	Rembrandt dates no painting this year.
1654	Hendrickje Stoffels, house-maid and Titus's nurse since the late '40s and living as Rembrandt's wife out of wedlock, is summoned for fornication. Her punishment: penance and banishment from celebrating the Lord's Supper.
1655	Rembrandt files for bankruptcy with a petition for "cessio bonorum"—losses at sea.
1656, July 25-26	"Inventory of paintings, including furniture and household effects" numbering nearly four hundred items catalogued and held for auction to cover Rembrandt's debts.
1658	Still faltering under financial troubles and debts, Rembrandt loses his house and moves with his family to a smaller rented home.
1663	The Black Death kills nearly ten thousand people in Amsterdam and, after a mild winter, returns and kills another twenty-four thousand, one-sixth of Amsterdam's population. Hendrickje is among the victims of the plague. Rembrandt stops painting almost entirely.
1665	Titus dies of the plague leaving his new wife, Magdelena, three months pregnant. Rembrandt hasn't enough money for a grave, so he rents a plot with the thought of moving his son's body later to a family plot. Titus is never moved.
1666	Titia, Rembrandt's granddaughter, is born. Her mother, Magdelena, dies seven months later.
1669	Rembrandt paints *Return of the Lost Son*, one of his last paintings.
1669, October 4	Rembrandt dies. Still short of money, he is buried somewhere in the Westerkerk in an unmarked and unrecorded grave.

"In writing a sequence on the life and work of Rembrandt, I envisioned a book that, while biographically accurate, is more than a biography in verse. My sequence also proposed to be more than a mere poetic gallery tour of the paintings. Rembrandt's life, known to us almost exclusively through the paintings and tantalizingly thin written documentation, is the stuff of real drama: he survived several plague outbreaks and the deaths of his two wives and four children. When he lost those he loved, he loved no less intensely, but more deeply and thoroughly. He enjoyed artistic triumphs and wealth, suffered unceremonious rejection and insolvency. Through all trials, Rembrandt remains in my sequence, as in the paintings, deeply human: flawed, burdened sympathetic, and frightfully, desperately honest about himself and others."

Stephen Frech holds degrees from Northwestern University, Washington University in St. Louis, and the University of Cincinnati. His manuscript, *Toward Evening and the Day Far Spent*, won the 1995 Wick Poetry Chapbook Contest and was published by Kent State University Press. His poems have apppeared in *The Georgia Review, Pleiades, Spoon River Poetry Review, Crab Creek Review, Ascent, Literary Review*, and others. He has been a recipient of the Elliston Poetry Writing Fellowship, the Milton Center Post-Graduate Writing Fellowship, a grant from the Ludwig Vogelstein Foundation, and an Illinois Arts Council Fellowship in Poetry

Author's photograph: Amy Gilman

THE WHITE PINE PRESS POETRY PRIZE

The annual White Pine Press Poetry Prize, established in 1995, offers a cash award plus publication of the winning manuscript. Manuscripts are accepted between July 15 and October 31 each year, and the winning manuscript is published the following spring. Please write for additional details.

2000   *If Not for These Wrinkles of Darkness* by Stephen Frech
        Selected by Pattiann Rogers

1999   *Trouble in History* by David Keller
        Selected by Pablo Medina

1998   *Winged Insects* by Joel Long
        Selected by Jane Hirshfield

1997   A *Gathering of Mother Tongues* by Jacqueline Joan Johnson
        Selected by Maurice Kenny

1996   *Bodily Course* by Deborah Gorlin
        Selected by Mekeel McBride

1995   *Zoo & Cathedral* by Nancy Johnson
        Selected by David St. John

About White Pine Press

Established in 1973, White Pine Press is a non-profit publishing house dedicated to enriching our literary heritage; promoting cultural awareness, understanding, and respect; and, through literature, addressing social and human rights issues. This mission is accomplished by discovering, producing, and marketing to a diverse circle of readers exceptional works of poetry, fiction, non-fiction, and literature in translation from around the world. Through White Pine Press, authors' voices reach out across cultural, ethnic, and gender boundaries to educate and to entertain.

To insure that these voices are heard as widely as possible, White Pine Press arranges author reading tours and speaking engagements at various colleges, universities, organizations, and bookstores throughout the country. White Pine Press works with colleges and public schools to enrich curricula and promotes discussion in the media. Through these efforts, literature extends beyond the books to make a difference in a rapidly changing world.

As a non-profit organization, White Pine Press depends on support from individuals, foundations, and government agencies to bring you important work that would not be published by profit-driven publishing houses. Our grateful thanks to the many individuals who support this effort as Friends of White Pine Press and to the following organizations: Amter Foundation, Ford Foundation, Korean Culture and Arts Foundation, Lannan Foundation, Lila Wallace-Reader's Digest Fund, Margaret L. Wendt Foundation, Mellon Foundation, National Endowment for the Arts, New York State Council on the Arts, Trubar Foundation, Witter Bynner Foundation, the Slovenian Ministry of Culture, The U.S.-Mexico Fund for Culture, and Wellesley College.

Please support White Pine Press' efforts to present voices that promote cultural awareness and increase understanding and respect among diverse populations of the world. Tax-deductible donations can be made to:

White Pine Press
P.O. Box 236, Buffalo, NY 14201